Pulse

poems
MELISSA FADUL

Raw Earth Ink

2023

This book is a work of poetry.

First paperback edition October 2023

Edited by Sharon Dolin and Candice Louisa Daquin

ISBN 978-1-960991-09-6 (paperback)

Published by Raw Earth Ink
PO Box 39332
Ninilchik, AK 99639
www.raw-earth-ink.com

For My Mother, My Father,
My Grandmothers, My Grandfathers
My Brother, the Giggle Magician
My Sister-In-Law
& My Niece

For Heather
I'll Always Hold Your Hand

To the Women I've Loved,
Who Have Loved Me,
Passed Through Me
& I've Passed Through

"When we contemplate the whole globe as one great dewdrop, ...flying through space with other stars all singing and shining together as one, the whole universe appears as an infinite storm of beauty."

John Muir

"The past is never where you think you left it."

Katherine Ann Porter

"You never really understand a person until you consider things from his point of view — until you climb into his skin and walk around in it."

Harper Lee

Table of Contents

Acknowledgements

Thank you to the editors of the magazines and anthologies below. Different versions of some of these poems have been published in the following:

As the World Burns: Writers and Artists Reflect on a World Gone Mad: "Hazard" and "Dodger, Black and White Snapshot, Ebbets Field, Brooklyn, 1955"

Killer Verse: Poems of murder and Mayhem: "Lord of Crows"

Negative Capability Press: "Tattooist's Needle, Jewish Museum"

Paumonok Interwoven: "To My Teenage Student In The Last Stage of Terminal Cancer"

Paumonok Transition: "Reverse Self-Portrait at Twelve" and "Somehow"

Pinecone Review: "After Our First Talk in Four Years," "The Woman Walking Through the Wind"

Setu Monthly Journal: "I've Been That Woman"

Smitten: This is What Love Looks Like: "Pulse" and "Do You Remember Christopher Street, June 1969?"

We Will Not Be Silenced: "She's Just an Elevator"

Due to the fact that these poems have gone through so many different personas, it's almost impossible to mention everyone who's helped me through the years to make this book come true. Without the guidance of the following people, I don't know how this baby would have been born:

Sharon Dolin, thank you for being the most extraordinary mentor and editor—For making me earn every syllable and never settling for less than the just the right word and for not allowing me to decide and use any other word than the best one for that particular line, stanza and poem—Thank you for always believing in my work and more significantly, me. Thank you for every critique and the hours spent toiling over my words—For pushing me even more than I already had been pushing myself to write outside of comfortability—for not only showing me how to enter that realm but stay in that place until I was ready to leave. Without knowing, you have showed me how to enhance my personal trust. Your encouragement is embedded within me indelibly. Lastly, thank you for trusting this book would happen and for telling me not to worry about writing a book, just write poems and the book will arise. Thank you to Emmeline Ortiz for your technological insight with the cover.

Thank you to the following amazing teachers I've been blessed to encounter and have throughout my life: Jeanne Marie Beaumont, Laure-Anne Bosselaar, the late Kurt Brown, Alexander Chee, Nicole Cooley, Mark Doty, Reagan Good, Terrance Hayes, Deborah Landau, Kathleen Ossip, Gregory Rabassa and my high school English teacher who said "Yes" the day I asked her if I could be a successful poet when I grow up. Thank you to all the great poets in Sharon Dolin's workshop: Patricia Behrens, Jeanne Blake, Charlotte Friedman, Vicki Iorio, Sarah Key, Elizabeth Lara, Ronnie Scharfman and Ellen Wright. I am grateful for the care and support all of you possess for my poetry and well-being.

Deep gratitude to my editor Candice Louisa Daquin. May we be moonsisters forever. Thank you for your relentless authenticity, empathy, patience and the rarest of kindness in a world too scared of even the slightest vulnerability. Your courage and strength is awesome. Thank you for believing and seeing my work for what it truly is when others did not. I am eternally grateful.

Thank you to my awesome and humane publisher, tara caribou of Raw Earth Ink. Your kindness, patience, and easy-going demeanor has always made me feel welcome and wanted. Thank you for always embodying ethical principles in an industry starving for it.

Most of all, thank you to my mother, father, brother, sister-in-law and niece, who have always supported this second life of mine—Lastly, thank you to my beautiful and incredible wife, Heather. Thank you for all your love, support, patience, and encouragement through the years—For always allowing me the solitude needed to write my truths in order to find home in my heart. You are my second heart. I Love You.

~Melissa

I.

Tattooist's Needle, Jewish Museum

I come from
women starving
for sleep —
chapped lips stuck
to deflated breasts.
A prisoner's palm,
clenched & closed
under his
control.
His fingers
steered me
where
to crawl,
dig & drag
through
convoys
of skin —
He taught
me the art
of etching
& scraping
numbers
into
arms.
I hold
drops
of
dried
blood
and
luck
on
my
tip.

I've Been that Kind of Woman

I've woken in jeans unzipped —
        bunched at my hips. Closed
when a guy grew too large to handle.

Opened to women who didn't love —
        tongues undeserving my taste never
found their way. I just teased with wetness.

Those days, it was all I could give
        even a decade after a stranger
forced his hands inside me.

Between the hour of coming & going

I'd get up and feel for my depression
        left in the mattress just to know I was
there. Drive until I found myself in some body

of water, where waves fell at my feet like nymphs
        mistaking me for a goddess —
pleading to kiss away their immortality.

I'd picture the only woman I made love to
        on a beach. She ran to the surf's lip,
wriggled out of clothes and screamed — *You coming?*

I slowed my pace to watch.
        Her figure waxed, the closer I came.
Low tide writhed against skin under moonlight.

Smirking, she called again — *Coming?*
        I undressed
and folded my arms across my chest.

She strolled to me dripping,
        dropped my hands:
You're so beautiful —

You have a body like Eve.
          Don't cover up,
don't ever hide.

It was months before I told her
          of being assaulted.
Adolescence spent hiding

in long sleeves, turtlenecks,
          jackets zipped up,
jeans even in July and August.

That night, her body
          was a bandage
drenched in tenderness.

The gauze of her tongue
          trailed my body.
We became another kind

          of enter.

I've Been Here Before

I come from fighting my mother
to wear a New York Mets shirt
and not a velvet dress

picture day in first grade.
I come from waves of cries
when she pushed

my arms through burgundy sleeves,
a doily collar scratched my neck.
I smiled at the camera anyway.

I come from my mom's afternoon whimpers
I'm sorry, I'm so sorry – I love you.
On my bed, my crinkled Mets shirt waited.

I come from resting my head on a baseball glove,
falling asleep at home
plate, pretending dirt was a blanket.

Stretching socks up legs like they were my wedding
stockings, sliding
pant sleeves over my knees.

I come from hours of death
stares — men & women
who at first, scowl and stop

to watch me in a cage
but smirk when I hit pitch after pitch
going 85 to 90 miles an hour.

At 43 years old,
strangers still warn: *Miss —*
you know that's really fast.

I come from inside wax packs. Find me
hugging a stick of gum, atop a mound
of cardboard baseball cards —

I come from neglected
natural skills
because I was a girl.

My little league coach
put me in right field
where boys never hit the ball.

I come from teaching myself
to catch fly balls
against the brick of my childhood home.

My father who tolerated the game,
threw me moonbeams
high enough to hit and pop clouds.

I come from my grandpa's
walk-up apartment — stories
above Brooklyn tracks he jumped over —

trolleys I wished I could've dodged
with him in *Pig Town*,
blocks from *Ebbets Field*.

I come from picturing myself, belonging —
a kid in the *Knothole Gang* —
searching for windows

in the outfield wall at *Ebbets* —
just for a peanut-sized peek
at the game.

I come from a hole in the fence
my brother axed
with a bat for us to slip through —

to our diamond we played on for years.
I come from watching out for cops.
My brother lifting just enough

of the broken & bent
fence for me to slide under —
so close to the earth,

even closer to the dirt of heaven.

Self Portrait at Twelve

Reverse the water's orbit
down the dark side of the drain
Reattach nails bitten past half-moons
Reverse the swelling of my inner thighs
Reverse the scalding water
Reverse his hands moving towards my body
Reverse his fingers thrusting
Reverse the waves bringing him closer
Reverse and stop the small talk
Reverse raising my mouth into a smile
Reverse his hurried legs that gained strength
shuffling through water to get to me
Reverse his thought that *hi* meant *come here*
Reverse the echo of hello

How You Set Me on Fire

We'd cut class to learn each other
without books or a lecture.
You'd jump in my car and I'd speed
to our favorite street.
Everyone was at work —
not one car in any driveway
Colonial houses on a wide road welcomed us.
Old oaks were soldiers
guarding against intruders.
Any of those houses could have been ours.
It was the brown brick home we dreamed of buying:
I saw myself in a robe on the turret balcony
blowing you kisses and waving goodbye
as you left each morn.
We spoke of painting the splintered gazebo,
must've had thirty conversations about colors —
still, the ending was always the same.
After the paint dried, we'd slow dance
to rain pitter pattering the roof.
Once, in the middle of our dreaming,
you turned your body sideways in the car,
laid your head on my thigh,
took my hand, pressed it to your chest and confessed,
I never felt this safe with any man.
I bent to kiss you,
before my lips even grazed yours,
you moaned into my mouth
setting me on fire.
You weren't ready for me —
my mouth and its inventions.
Instead, we got out of the car
and walked to the dried-up well
in front of "our" house and
screamed down,
I love you, I love you, I love you.

She's Just an Elevator

temporary transport
        away from the marriage
of suits and lies to a lobby in a motor inn.

Some guy pays to enter.
        The owner ignores her face
that doesn't match her picture ID.

He winks & hands the nameless a key
        to a cabin whose floors are congealed
in boot prints of other Johns.

Bugs move between plaster & wallpaper,
        same as her daughter reading Braille—
fingers swimming across the page's pool

like a typewriter carriage before its ding
        sings, *you got a second? Get out of this now.*
Cold hands jolt her back,

bend and hoist her over a table
        garnished with fake roses caked in dust.
Pressing her face into the wood over&over,

he's in a hurry to get back to work
        she's the up and down button
that will make him come faster.

She tries to ignore her worn and sore shaft
        with thoughts of her daughter
before cancer took her daughter's vision.

        This helps her open
for seconds then slowly seal herself
        with a stranger inside.

Motel Mirror

Before the pregnant woman removed
her clothes, she looked into me,
like she was a fortune teller and I, a crystal ball.
She sighed and whispered, how do I do this?
I could only offer reflection—
truth—its careful inventions.
She ran a finger down one of my cracks,
pressed a hand to my glass face,
stripped and waited for her boyfriend
who was skimming a textbook.

After patting and brushing her swollen stomach,
he looked at the catheter in his hand.
After insertion, a flood of blood—he ran
to get towels from the bathroom then left her.
With hands, I would've tried to build a dam,
some barrier for the hemorrhaging.
With fingers, I could've dialed 911.
I watched her pull sheets from the bed,
stuff them between her legs to block the blood.
She bent before me—
a woman on her knees without a prayer.

I Am a Jew

hath not a Jew eyes　　　　　who silently wept
hath not a Jew hands　　　　that carried corpses,
organs, dimensions　　　　　to and from ovens —
senses, affections, passions　over time ended up numb
hurt with the same weapons　flogged — but I didn't cry
subject to the same diseases　burnt and experimented on
healed by the same means　　Was death a blessing?
If you prick us, do we not bleed?　I asked the Kapo tattooing forearms.
If you tickle us, do we not laugh?　Yes. A blessing I cannot afford
If you poison us, do we not die?　We looked up at all the fleshy smoke
If you wrong us, shall we not revenge?　He said, learn to turn revenge's cheek

Elegy for My Mother's Aborted Fetus, from Your Pro-Choice Sister

Dearest, it's taken over forty years to write you.
Ma doesn't
talk about you

often.
Once, when I was a teen,
she said, the doctor wouldn't tell me its sex.

He said, it's just a fetus —
Go home —   Forget it —
she said, rubbing her stomach.

Would you have been my older sister?
Understood why I was a tomboy
and told me it was ok

that I didn't like dresses as a kid?
Stuck up for me when Ma
put me in one on school picture day?

Would you have beaten up the boy
who made fun of blue & burgundy shoes
I wore to correct pigeon-toed feet?

Would you have been home when I got my first period?
Showed me how to use the tampon,
brought me a heating pad for my cramps?

Would you have modeled how to put on a bra,
pushed my chest closer together
to create more cleavage.

Would you have said like Ma,
you have such a good figure.
You have my body before I was pregnant.

I don't recall ever looking at myself
closely, until I started dating a woman
who had never seen a naked woman up close.

I remember her eyes turning to fingers
traversing curves where my skin dipped.
She whispered — you have a body like Eve

and bent down to let her mouth
dance around my stomach
as I covered it with my hand.

Quarantine Prayer, 2020

Let my mother's fingers
curl around the kettle's handle,
as water falls from the faucet

into the steamer's open mouth.
I hope pent-up strength in her hands
is able to pull the door open

and grab the jug of milk for tea.
Let her smile when she lifts
the lid to find cream pooled.

Let her lips still want to kiss my father
when he moves in close
wishing her good morning.

I hope his legs bend without arthritic fire
running through his feet
when they wiggle into slippers

under the table. Let them
take up their forks,
exchange dreams from the night.

I hope my mother laughs harder than before
when she tells my dad she dreamt again
of peeling potatoes with my grandmother.

After, let her head upstairs
where she'll open hope's chest
to hold her mother's peeler.

Will my father reach for the negative
of a photo — my teenage mother
posing on a park bench?

I yearn for the Harley
he never bought
to rev and blow off collected dust.

Let him wipe years of webs
off my brother's hockey stick
and my baseball bat—

while day's last dollop of light slips through the shutter's slats.

To the Man Behind the Bar

Return the gin — unpour the liquid fire, bartender.
God, he's in and out of consciousness on your bathroom tile.
Dump the *Big Gulp* cup you fill up free for my father.

If you're his friend sir, why pour him more or even let him enter?
He drove drunk last night over the bridge while vomiting bile.
Return the gin — unpour the liquid fire bartender.

I've seen him swaddled and bound to a stretcher,
his body too wide for the gurney — 911, on redial.
I've dumped the *Big Gulp* cup you fill up free for my father.

His ulcer's a butcher chopping his insides with a cleaver.
In the emergency room, his eyes seemed to roll back a mile.
Return the gin — unpour the liquid fire, bartender.

When he woke, there was nothing he remembered.
His doctor asked, do you drink sir? He said, not in a long while.
Again, I dumped a *Big Gulp* cup you fill up free for my father.

He signed a contract I drew up to go to therapy — to try to stay sober.
He left without the paper promise — this was how he reconciled.
Return the gin — unpour the liquid fire, Father.
Dump the *Big Gulp* cup you fill up free of charge.

My mother says, *tell me through poetry what you're afraid of*

wrinkles lining your palms
age taking your arms
dotting them with spots

Your mane going
from strawberry to salt
you blowing out another year's flame

Holding me close enough to feel
enveloped by heat but not far enough
to not discern the burning

Dropping you off home
letting you limp and go
through darkness

watching you lean on your less
arthritic leg for leverage
allowing you to struggle

on steps I've gone down
more than up
Trusting the night light

will sense your flesh
& flicker on as you turn
the key & push in — the doorway

framing you as you turn
back to me, your smudged
handprint on the glass

Elegy for My Youth

Are monkey bars still waiting for me to climb—
does the turtle shell's sprinkler still spout water,
like some cloud on the ground burst open?

I think my brother and I can still make believe
our playground is a diamond.
Race to the water fountain turned first base.

Can I pretend the seal statue has remained
second? Will my arms reach a rainbow,
where third base is our golden retriever?

Let my mother sit on a wooden bench
legs stretched out, reading *Women's Day*
or *Good Housekeeping*.

Let her be Home.

Would my brother still try to blow heaters by me when I bat?
Let people stop to ask,
where did you learn to hit like that?

Where are the ancient oaks—
our gloveless fielders,
whose leaves waved and clapped from the outfield?

Let my brother grin running out of the park
like he just swallowed the sun's rays,
when my mother screams, *You want ice cream?*

Does the giant cone on the shop's roof
still twirl and swirl
like a belly dancer?

Please let the Carvel bell ding
when we step and push
open the door.

Would the owner who served us, still
be there — wearing a paper hat,
rolling a chocolate chip globe into a cone?

Can someone tell me where I left my giggles
after he shook a spoonful of sprinkles
over the scoop?

Will my brother still let chocolate
drip and stain his shirt while my mother
wipes and bites into her butter pecan?

Riding home, let my mother's humming
lull my brother to rest his head
on my shoulder —

his knees grass-stained,
chocolate ice cream stuck to his cheeks,
our shared glove napping in my lap —

my hand gripping the only baseball we didn't lose.

II.

Dysthymia

If my brain were
the inside of a blood orange,
and my skull the rind,
I could peel back its skin
and sink my fingers into the fruit —
palm, squeeze and juice my brain,
until it all falls
between the folds of my fingers
filling my glass of emptiness —
and under the moons of my fingernails
the pulp of happiness —
I'd drink myself.

After Our First Talk in Four Years

Memory rewound our discussion, your words,
I'm open if you want to meet face-to face.
I couldn't

tell you I still love you — not like lovers
in a field of barley camouflaging their bodies.
It's graciousness — you're still a well holding my secrets.

If one were to drain your depths
I still think you wouldn't give up those secrets.
Over the line, I didn't know how to say,

it took years for transference's burn to bronze and fade.
Even now if someone calls your name, I stop. Hope
and not hope you're near,

so temptation doesn't blurt,
tell me one of your stories —
this heart has starved

Remind me of the real
matter — let your body
lean into its shadow

when you tell me of a couple
whose infant died —
who pulled off the freeway

after the funeral
unbuckled
the baby's car seat

and dumped it on the shoulder.
Hours later they went back to find it
gone.

The Woman Walking Through the Wind

tucking her curls behind her ears,
looked like you only for a breeze—

still, your words during a rendezvous
years ago, rose in me:

Our bond is so much more
than anything sexual.

Wanderlust's draft
aroused dormant wishes

again, to travel you—
wonder once more

could we ever share bodies—
not just thoughts trapped in stories?

How would it feel to wake
in the bed to dawn's first glints,

shadows slipping
through shutters like love letters

sliding into envelopes?
Turning in time

to watch you bid for a bit more rest—
wrestling to open sleepy eyes—

straddling the seam
of this world and dream

but awake enough
to press yourself into my lips.

Kintsugi

From across a restaurant, I thought I saw you—
a woman's blond locks curled at her shoulders
like a snail huddled in its shell.

She turned to me.
Did she sense my eyes on her?
It's not your face—

but one spoiled
by age's blade
not beauty—

a different kind of erosion.
Someday, in my waking life
I might understand why

I still search for you
in places I know
your heart would fit—

Why I still stop
to look through reflections
in revolving doors.

Hunt for you in an ocean
of restless, rushed figures
I brush on the subway.

Scour hotel rooms
thinking I will find you
folding old baby clothes,

before leaving them
on a cool pillow for maids
to take because they're not paid enough.

Would you remember telling me that?
The last time we spoke you reminded me
you're old and your memory is dead.

I need you to know that at most,
I can only go months without
thinking of you.

We know each other
almost twenty years
but have no photos together.

As if I were an expensive porcelain dish
fractured, and you
golden glue

meant to show me
not how to mend
but that I can.

Sometimes you broke as well
even though you weren't supposed to
shatter in front of me.

I couldn't help
but build you
makeshift splints

I glued with golden sap,
and wood axed from the last
standing tree of my childhood.

Movieworld Where I Saw *Field of Dreams*, Closes

The marquee is missing —
there's no one in black and white
to put up new film titles by hand.

Nothing but negative space
fills frames to display the latest flicks.
Someone kicked in the glass — it's ruptured, but not broken.

Through a prism of cracks, no popcorn machine lid
is being pushed up by jumpy kernels,
ready to dive into a bucket filled with butter.

Construction workers didn't roll the carpet
after tearing it up. It lies clumped like a corpse
in the fetal position at the center of the lobby.

A stranger took a heat gun to the wallpaper,
until it wilted and melted.
It drapes like a face desperate for good news.

On a pillar, drip drops of paint
cover Gene Kelly's silhouette,
fedora and his open umbrella.

My eyes wet with yesterday
try to reach for the brass banister, gone.
A doorless corridor leads to the theatre where I sat

on my legs at ten in a creaky seat to see over a stranger.
Shoeless Joe Jackson's ghost strolled through corn stalks
to a baseball field built by a farmer named Ray

who plowed his corn and created a diamond
after a vision and voice
told him, *if you build it, he will come* —

I've always just gone with the dream:
building a baseball field, to bring back
his father's hero.

Even though I don't like it when bankrupt Ray
leaves his wife & daughter to hunt the voice
telling him to ease his pain, I cheer for him---

like when I root for myself in those unreal hours
trying to be that selfish — that human
wishing for my dead to rise from dreams.

Ray turns up hundreds of miles from home
on the doorstep of his favorite writer
who's washed up for decades.

Even after he fakes a finger in his coat pocket is a gun,
almost gets hit with a crowbar by the pacifist poet
and kidnaps the writer to a game at *Fenway,*

I stick with this story — waiting
for anything that tips the balance
of the mundane in favor of the surreal.

Some nights, I still walk the distance
listening to one streetlamp sputtering hope.
In second-hand stores, I dust off calendars,

searching for 1989
wishing the world would go
back in time to when I was young.

I can only plead with the moon to light
up the ghosts of those I've lost —
bright as a movie marquee

before they vanish or get close enough to reach out for me.

Baseball

Calf flesh sewn with sutures
formed into a horseshoe.
Your seams taught
me how to hold,
grasp the world
A family of string
strung around a rubber core.
My young girl's palm
wouldn't get much bigger
than your orb.
I prayed my fingers
would become longer,
strong enough to grip
and dig into your skin
when throwing
a proper knuckleball.
Dug my nails as deep
as they'd go
toward your center
until their moons turned
pink then red.
When I wound up
and threw your mini globe,
I tried to keep my mind
and body compact
extending myself
through the crevice
of a window crack
I invented.

Driving Until I Find a Diamond

with players to forget the world
of cancer that could show up on my mom's
next ultrasound,

I spot a field and get out of my car.
Guys stop what they're doing to watch me
walk to the grandstand and slide into a bleacher —

It's the first live game I've been to in a year and a half
since Covid's pandemic hit.
Doesn't matter that it's softball — not baseball,

nor the *Yankees* or *Mets* playing
or that I'm not in my hometown, *Queens,*
but *Long Island* — it's close enough.

These men are my father's age —
in their seventies — running the bases like boys
chasing summer's ghost as it flies into fall's knothole.

Their hands don't shake like my dad's
whenever he holds a phone, a cup or anything.
Maybe one of them has an alcohol problem, like my father —

I can't tell. The guy with bad knees still manages
to step into a slider and drive the ball to the outfield.
In between pitches, they joke from the dugout

about their empty retirement homes in Florida,
boats docked in *Safe Harbor,*
and the yachts they can't afford

yet. One man bitches about a wart on his finger,
and I think of motor oil etched into the heartlines
of my blue-collar father's palms.

How they resemble a route
with no memory —
a place with no alcohol,

no cancer —
where I can't recall new cuts,
his blood on the lock and doorknob.

A haven where he doesn't
scrub his hands with WD40
to get the car oil off his lifelines.

Where the black isn't
packed so tight, so deep
under his thumbnails covering the moons.

Another earth where everyone knows my father's
fingerprints under hoods of engines
he brought back to life.

His prints protected, caked over by the dust of years.

When I Go

For my brother and niece

bury all of me
except fingers & toes.
Turn those digits to ashes.

Throw them into our park's lake.
Grip them like the baseballs
you once pitched to me.

Run around the invented
bases. After your palm hugs the bat,
roll your fingers around its handle.

Let memory line up door-knocker knuckles,
swing, and look into your daughter's eyes
after her slider slides past you.

Give her the glove we shared for decades,
Put it in the core of her palm —
your hand over hers.

Direct the ball towards its deep
oiled seams
where childhood sleeps.

Dodger in Black & White, World Series, Yankee Stadium, 1955

I could have been the one
      filming Robinson
sneaking down third.
      His spikes pounding the powdered foul line.
It could have been me
      rooting for Jackie as he jet home,
his cotton pants like dove wings.
      I wasn't alive to see him dive
around the masked catcher,
      his hand sliding across the base.
Could it ever have been me —
      my handprint on home plate,
hoping the umpire screams,
      SAFE?

Blind Woman Walking Along the Strand to Synagogue

My wife says, *I love this window — I picture you*
watching the blind woman
that's your neighbor —

you have an aerial view of her.
I know you wait to make sure
she gets to shul safely.

Saturdays, I wake early and lean on the pane
to watch if the blind woman has gone to pray.
Grateful the days she appears — elderly Aphrodite

molded from starlight,
donning a 1940s burgundy
victory suit.

Her jacket with black buttons
outlines her less than hour-glass figure.
An A-line skirt always lags a bit —

like a constant breeze she seems
to have dragged from the camps during liberation.
A maroon tam hat sits sideways on her head,

brunette hair held together in a silk snood.
When she walks the cobblestone path
the heels of her pumps wobble.

Climax, Teaching Elie Wiesel's *Night*

I ask, should Elie eat his dying father's food?

There's nothing you can do.   John with terminal cancer says.
You can't think of others   Imagine
trying to survive *Auschwitz*   only worrying about yourself
Luke interrupts John—   *But he's your father.*
You're crazy   What do you know—

you don't know what it's like to be dying.

Our Naked Hour

Let me in
the way only

a wife can
let in a wife.

Forgive your body
if it tenses against mine,

when the ghost of assault probes
our naked hour.

You are the only one
who can pull your hurt up by its roots.

When you're ready
imagine my body a harbor

for your orphan tears.

My kisses will water—
grow you new

skin, without
the wound of memory.

Alams for Depression during the Covid Pandemic, Ten Months In

I can't hear   I can't bear   not to look
    another   one more   body
       ambulance   stretcher   gone

Stay   away   six   feet   apart
   I can't   survive   lacking
     hug   smiles   masked

Before We Divorce

Come home to me
once more. I'll leave

the light on.
Turn the key in our lock, push —

our dogs'll be barking,
their tails metronoming.

I'll be there — waiting,
leftover kisses on my lips —

in the depression
of the love seat.

Hold me
once more.

Remember me
running up behind you

on our wedding day, arms
laced around each other?

In your eyes, I can still see
the shore we visited one Valentine's Day.

When we kissed, you shut
the veil of your lids,

hiding cobalt pearls.

III.

Pulse

To them, we're already just bodies on the floor
Dancing then shot dead
Not making it out freedom's door.

We're cooled by the same water ebbing at the shore.
Like them, we get scared of corpses drenched in red —
They're *us* — those bodies on the floor.

We dream of a day we won't have to say anymore:
Next could be me or the woman I chose to wed
Not making it out freedom's door.

Holding hands, we choose to fight this war,
my lips pressed against her skin in our bed.
To them, we're already just bodies on the floor.

I'm not damned or in need of a cure
I really don't require conversion — instead
Know this: I'm worthy of walking through freedom's door.

Even when living becomes less thrill than chore.
We won't bleed and bleed until all blood is bled —
We're not just bodies on the floor,
We'll dance through and out freedom's door.

Do You Remember Christopher Street, June 1969?

I was the first woman to throw a stone at your head

before you shackled me and spotted blood on your palms, before

you swung your baton, thumped my skull —

do you have nightmares about me pleading,

please loosen the cuffs — they're cutting my wrists?

I swear, stars bled and wept light through my lashes —

do you still think of my breasts —

your fingers squeezing them

when you shoved me in the patrol wagon,

do you recall licking the red

streaking down your cheeks

on the floorboard gelling with mine

when you slammed the door —

I thought I was unable to watch

one more cop chuck another one of us

face first against the car — until the thud —

one more body thunder thumped against the iron prowler —

I couldn't stop my head from popping up,

glaring through the porthole — eyes fastened on mine,

Can you recollect the clunk of my pumps' heels

beating in the door to divert you — she squawked,

that *is* ME, that is *my* ID,

Her ID dropped when you bounced her against the car again.

Do you recall your paw palming her head against the window —

When you force-frisked her — I whispered, *mercy*

imagining my cuffed hand free to press against hers.

Lord of Crows

In a meadow of forget-me-nots,
a farmer bucks barley
in Wyoming dark.

Inside a chicken coop, his son
chooses eggs. He picks the best
blackberries for breakfast from a bush.

The boy runs into the house,
slams the screen door behind him.
He drops an egg. His mother mutters: *no yolk?*

Two miles west,
in Laramie, a bartender
wipes the bar,

counts his tips and looks
at his rusted trailer home out the window.
A stray cat rustles through garbage.

Juke box belts,
I'll be
what I am.

Two men play pool.
Another introduces himself
as Matthew.

He buys both a round.
Soon, the three set out
together.

In a pickup truck,
a beer bottle rocks
back, forth on the floor,

striking Matthew's feet.
Next to him,
a bible, barbed wire.

They drive to a deserted field
maybe filled
with forget-me-nots,

rob Matthew of his wallet,
shoes, and pistol whip him.
They bind

his ninety-eight pound frame
to a fence
with barbed-wire and run

into him with the truck —

Leave.

Eighteen hours later:

A crow pecks at his
straw-like hair, slipping
on his dented bloody skull,

a farmer picks the day's spuds.
A child rides his bike
after blackberries and eggs.

He mistakes Matthew for a scarecrow.

Rockefeller Center, December 2019

Towering over the plaza, Prometheus
        holds his fire in a fennel stalk, guarding
couples sailing around the ice rink.

Gusts sharp as arrowheads push me
        toward the unveiling:
a chopped down tree

dolled up in tinsel mascara, ornaments
        resembling wrecking balls
and a girdle of garland,

when I spot her space
        where she begged
twenty-seven years ago.

I see the imprint of a body
        on the wall where she leaned.
Is that what's left of her —

the way the ghost
        of a picture always remains
where it used to hang?

I can still see her wearing nothing
        but a Glad bag.
Holes cut out for arms and head.

Knees pressed to chest,
        arms hugging legs.
On the ground, a Dixie cup, rocking.

It's been years
        since I've dragged her from childhood.
Frozen —

similar to when I first saw her
        without my wallet,
I couldn't give her anything.

I settled for shared shivers — currents
        passed through us
like lightning forking a tree trunk.

My father's voice,
        Let's go,
jolted me out of her world.

He grabbed my hand —
        I dawdled glancing at her
and prayed to whatever gods:

Make me magical enough
        to steal Prometheus' stolen flames —
strong enough to melt the gilded gold

with my breath
        and brave enough
to hand her a bouquet of fire.

Show and Tell, Black and White Photograph, Mississippi, 1945

Church-quiet pupils,
huddle like crows
in the throat of a bell,
before its tonsil tolls.
A boy's eyes
prowl the clock
anxious to unfold
the only picture
he has of his father—
hanging.

Teenage Boy on Bicycle Killed by a Sniper, Doctor Late to Scene

Forgive me.
    I didn't
show up in your room —

I was not the doctor
    I was supposed to be.
I wasn't there

early enough
    to hold his head when a bullet
exploded in his brain.

Forgive me — I hit snooze
    to spoon my lover a bit longer —
silenced news alerts on TV.

Forgive me — let me bury him
    in the coffin
of my voice box.

Forgive my relief
    when I learned it wasn't
my son's blood

embedded in threads of rubber tires.
    Forgive me for keeping
the victim's notebook

I wrote a love note
    to his parents
with a bloodied pencil and left

it between the wheels' gold spokes.
    I hugged his sandals
to my chest as if they were my son's.

Forgive the bullet that gutted his skull —
    the government that forced me
to barter my stethoscope for a burqa.

In the Navel of the Moon

My student who reads *The Odyssey*
        over and over for pleasure
refuses to leave after class.

Eyes dark as the Nile
        dilate into loneliness.
She mouths, *I'm lonely. I can't write.*

She says, *this is all I have*
        and pushes her journal in front of me.
It's not very good. I'm clogged.

Docked in the center of the page, a small boat
        flows and floats
through watery white.

I ask, is this the boat that brought you
        to America —
that rocks in the harbor of your dreams?

Can you hear it still creaking —
        planks of wood that groaned at night
when you slid from your mother's arms

and crept to the bow to convince water to take you back —
        where you hop-scotched barefoot
under a clothesline, in a T-shirt filled with the day's soil?

Can you still see the sleeve tear and fall from
        your shoulder when you climbed the church wall
to watch the nuns put on their habits?

Do you think you could ever step again where summer tasted
        like air-dried laundry, and you sang in English,
but counted in Spanish?

Can you feel the sun lightly toasting your skin?
　　　Do you remember your mother rubbing feet
scratched by dirt before you traded soil

for New York concrete? I know you
　　　recall the story behind the scar
you caress for comfort—

the fall from the footbridge you fished on
　　　with a string tied to a stick.
Show me how hard it was

to catch a bite without bait,
　　　and how easy it is not to
in America at seventeen.

Mateo

A new student, whose name means gift from God,
wants me to call him M.
Mateo, who claims he watched his uncle get shot.

Mateo, who sat in his uncle's blood
until the ambulance came.
Mateo, who I'm trying to teach to say uncle

instead of putting up his fists.
Who won't work for any other teacher.
When I ask him what is more powerful:

love or hate—
writes something like, I believe hate
is more powerful—

love can make you vulnerable—
if the girl leaves you,
then you have nobody.

Mateo, who would fight the world
and throw up his fists
if a stranger hurt someone he loves—

doesn't listen to some others
because they scream at him
for entering the library without permission.

When the teachers call on me for help,
I just giggle while chasing him
in the biography section,

knowing he'll duck
into an empty shelf.
He'll pull his legs to his heart.

like a kid in an abandoned tire,
waiting
to be pushed.

In the sideways Yankees cap his brother gave him,
he smirks when I sing, I found you
and puts his hand out for me to pull him up.

Mateo, who has two cop investigations pending
for beating a kid bloody in the park.
Who loves stickers and smiles through his mask

and yells, Wow —
when I say, *Great work!*
Mateo, who grinned a little more

than usual when I shouted, it's good to see you.
after he was away for a month.
He muttered quickly, it's good to see you too.

While on vacation, he rode a zipline
wearing a loose harness
with nothing but rock below,

told me, it's different there.
I had to stop the zipline with my hands.
It was weird. But I wasn't scared.

That week he came to school four days straight.
When he came back, he said, *Miss, I had to*
wash my family's laundry.

But I didn't have enough money,
so the owner made me leave
all our clothes until I could pay.

Mateo, who by June could have a ninety in my class
and a tracking bracelet from the cops
around his ankle.

Mateo who is always hungry—
knows I won't mark him late on days
he gets a bacon, egg and cheese before class.

Who went into Taco Bell one afternoon
and came out in cuffs—
Who says, *Don't worry*

when I say, *Please be safe*
have a good weekend—
be careful.

Mateo, who didn't run out to play in the snow
when the last bell of the day rang
but stayed in the school lobby

with me and said, Miss, it's scary out there.
Mateo whose way of saying goodbye
is making gang signs with his fingers

and asking me to mimic him.
Who just bows his head & says, yes, ma'am,
when I say stop talking to the girls & get back to class.

Mateo who once came running,
screaming my name
down the hall into my room holding his stomach,

begging me to write him
a lunch pass
because he said, *I'm starving.*

Somehow

Somehow, she manages to step downstairs
while she makes room
for pain bulging under her skin.
Through nausea & dizziness,
somehow she sleeps
through drives to chemo.
Somehow, she sits for four hours with a tube
projecting from her vein and does homework.
Today, in a pandemic, she's writing
her college essay for my class. Somehow, she is able
to tell me—a woman she really doesn't know,
how doctors found cancer
while sick with covid.
Somehow, she is here
to relive it on paper.
When the pouch has run out
of poison to infuse her,
somehow, she stands and walks white-walled halls
without her father holding her.
Later, somehow she attends school over computer.
Somehow, she stays up, aware—
doesn't let herself lose focus.
I believe I will somehow watch her walk
at the end of the year across the stage
and shake our principal's hand. Somehow,
she will turn to find her parents in the crowd clapping,
while she throws her arm in the air and pumps a fist to the
heavens.

Hazard

Because my students wear hoodies
in the rain. Because they run
out of their houses to 7-Eleven
pursuing Skittles and iced tea cravings.
At the park, a cop threw Andrew against a brick wall
because he fit a suspect's description—
the can of Arizona iced tea in his pocket
popped and ran down his leg like urine
when someone's nervous.
Because it could have been Arnold
who is on a full ride to college, hit with a bullet
in the stomach while swallowing rainbow candies—
I could see Mike sprint away because he's scared
someone is following him—not because he did anything.
It could have been his blood running down a sewer drain,
mixing with Skittles dye—his candy and corpse
covered with sand after the body was pronounced dead.
It could have been Ron, who asked me before the Ferguson riots,
Why do blacks still sit in the back of the bus
if they don't have to anymore?
I asked him, *Do you?*
He just looked down at his desk.
The other day, my oldest friend's husband, Derek
repeated, *That could've been me just taking a jog —*
I could've have been shot.
I asked him, *Are you scared*
to go for a run now?

Not where we live – other places, yes.

I added, *My love*

is from Kentucky,

while it's not the same,

there are counties like Hazard

where we couldn't even hold hands

or order a wedding cake.

Prejudice is prejudice, he responded.

In the background, my oldest friend,

Nicole yells, *White privilege.*

A week later, a witness records an officer kneeling

on the neck of a black man

lying on his stomach for over nine minutes

before an ambulance came.

If I would have tried

to stop the cop, would I

have been tasered? Shot?

It could have been

my friends Mark or Derek.

It could have been

me at Derek's funeral —

my arms around Nicole

trying to hug the hurt out of her.

How Many Lion-Hearted

goodly creatures
are there here
How beauteous
our *mankind is*
O' brave new world
We are such stuff
our little life waiting
to be sung by soil

heard mercy's gavel slam
in the Pied Piper's courtroom
hired guns,
lay down arms for alms
We're light yearning to be found
as dreams are made on
some night song
rounded with sleep

six feet deep.

Alzheimer's Waltz

twinkle twinkle little

Sara — how does it —

"star, grandma." "Star."

Grandma, my name's Melissa, remember?

Sara, where is your father?

"Outside with Uncle Michael."   *Twinkle*

twinkle (

)what is it again?

"little star"   *Sara, do you believe in God?*

I'm hungry. Can we have lunch Sara?

"Just did, remember? I baked you a cake for your birthday." *It's my birthday?*

"Yeah. Should be done in like five minutes."

— In 1985,

Jesus came to me when I was sleeping one night

"Yea, what did he look like?"   *He had long*

hair and wore a (   ) twinkle twinkle little,

where is your father?

"He's outside with uncle Michael."

"Where was Jesus when he came to you, grandma?"   *Who?*

"JESUS — CHRIST — He's dangling from your neck."

He wore all

white, (wait…

{pointer finger u-turns, taps the brim of her chin}

[63]

(   ) *had no feet and just*

    floated

I'm dizzy can we stop   for a moment. Where's my cranberry juice?

{She reaches for the glass next to her and it crashes to the floor}

        I'm sorry. Can we go to the Automat for dinner?

{I bend to cleanup up the spill}

"grandma, why did you pee on yourself and the floor?

How come you didn't tell me you had to go?"

        I didn't know I went.
    Sara do you have a boyfriend?(

"No grandma.")

[Should I remind her of my sexuality?]

        How's your "friend?"

[funny what she does keep in mind, huh?]

"She um-we broke up a while ago."

    Do you have a boyfriend? Sara, when I was 18,

        I sang in The Waldorf Astoria and Charlie Chaplin
        was there. Do you know what he said to me?

"I forgot."

[I let her go even though I've heard this story over and over]

    He asked, are all Greek girls as beautiful as you?

"What do you like to sing grandma?"   *Twinkle Twinkle little—*

    Sara--I forgot   the rest.

"I know."   *Where's my husband? Sara, where is my husband?(*

        "Grandpa isn't here.")

                        Where is he?

"The cemetery."   *Why? Who died?*

"He did."   *When?*

"About twenty three years ago. I'm going to the bathroom, be right back."

{I come back into the room} "So, you think that cake's ready yet?"

   Who are you?   You look like my granddaughter Tell me your name.

{Phone rings} Hi. Ma. Everything's fine. But she asked me who I was

when I came back from the bathroom. *Sara, who was the woman here before?* Hold on Ma.   *She looked like your sister, Sara.*

{I hang up the phone}

"That was me grandma. I don't have a sister." *Oh.*

                I forget a lot. Don't I? Twinkle, Twinkle, Sara, sing

the rest — "little star, how I wonder what you are."

To the First Terminally Ill Student I Taught

Swing from a Wisconsin Willow
Not gone is the stream
where frogs still leap

and tease mosquitoes in a brook
Flip from the tire swing into the creek
to impress your best friend

She's the one you long to love and don't
know why
Bounce a stone off water to trigger ripples

When she asks if you're lonely
remind her you don't have time to feel that
beautiful

Stumble with tumbleweed
pirouetting over railroad tracks
On a hay bank mimic a mockingbird's iambs

Blow dandelions to dust
Chase a rabbit through a maze of cabbage
Make yourself a bed of leaves & fall

asleep under an apple tree
with your dog
the shortest day of the year

Savor cherries you stole from the grove
Lean a seed on your mouth's crown
roll it with the rug of your tongue

Let your smile dwell
on windmill wings
Linger on a branch

worn by ranchers
who stop for the night to rest
their barrel bodies on sycamore bark

Join them when they rise
and flood the aqueduct with gulls
hunting for flapping salmon

And, if you must go—

go when summer is

least—

when fall has bled its last brown

before earth strips into the bare season

wrapping and marooning you

in a cocoon of leaves.

There's a Funeral in Me Missing

Grandma, the day you died
I moved into a London hotel
waiting for workers to paint my apartment.

I was another kind of canvas.

The day of your funeral, it rained —
I spilled into a reflection
across Atlantic's pond.

Sat on the steps
of the British museum
you once ran up excited.

When strangers closed
their umbrellas, canopies
collapsed, like roses folding.

Your umbrella painting
hangs in my writing room.
There's something

about all those umbrellas being
open at once — close together
twirling in mid-air:

Pinwheel guards
protecting the heavens,
from our sky's rough edges.

You told me your secret
about the one in the corner
in the teal patch of puddle.

It was just a reflection
having the last word.

Notes

"I am a Jew", "Climax, Teaching Elie Wiesel's Night" and "How Many Lion-Hearted" embody the contrapuntal form. The contrapuntal form braids two plus poems together. Thus, creating one poem that can be read a few ways on the page. The inspiration for the form comes from Tyehimba Jess' collection, "Olio." Thank you, Mr. Jess.

The italicized words in the poem "I am a Jew" come from Shakespeare's play *The Merchant of Venice*.

"How You Set Me on Fire" is for D.

In the poem "Dysthymia" dysthymia/persistent depressive disorder is defined as a low grade mild form of depression that lasts for a minimum of two years.

In the poem "Kintsugi" the word kintsugi translates to golden repair. It is an ancient Japanese art in which people repair pottery using golden lacquer mixed with glue. The golden lacquer is meant to highlight the pottery's breaks and flaws.

"Movieworld Where I Saw *Field of Dreams*, Closes" is for my mother.

In the poem "Climax, Teaching Elie Wiesel's *Night*" the italicized text is excerpted from Elie Wiesel's memoir *Night*.

In the poem, "Alams for Depression during the Covid Pandemic, Ten Months In" Alams are defined as brief poems originally written and sung by Bedouin poets who lived in eastern Libya and western Egypt.

"Teenage Boy on Bicycle Killed by a Sniper, Doctor Late to Scene" is after Annie Liebovitz's photograph, *Fallen bicycle of teenage boy just killed by a sniper, Sarajevo, 1994.*

The meaning behind the title of the poem "In the Navel of the Moon" is as follows: The word Mexico comes from the indigenous people, the Náhua. Mexico is a Nahuatl term derived from Metztli meaning "moon" and xictli which means navel or center. It alludes to the Aztecs who built Tenochtitlán in the middle of the lake of the moon.

"Somehow" is for E.

"Hazard" is for N, D, & M.

The italicized words in the poem "How Many Lion-Hearted" come from Shakespeare's play *The Tempest*.

"To the First Terminally Ill Student I Taught" is for J.T.

Praise for *Pulse*

From the first poem in Melissa Fadul's remarkable *Pulse*, where a tattoo needle speaks of its shattering past during the Holocaust, to poems that express the way assault and lesbian desire commingled in memory, these poems are searing in their honesty about what it is to live fully in the truth of being a queer Jewish woman in America today. This is a brave book that risks everything to do as Adrienne Rich asserted: "When a woman tells the truth, she is creating the possibility for more truth around her." And the truth Fadul tells, in poems crafted and profound and at times tender, speaks to all of us. What an audacious and brilliant debut!

    —Sharon Dolin, author of *Imperfect Present*

Poet Melissa Fadul writes from a deeply witnessed perspective that evokes the very soul of childhood in her debut collection *Pulse*. Alongside masterful poetic-storytelling. Fadul weaves her witness of private histories and truth, whilst shaping words and phrases of incomparable beauty that pour into a mesmerizing story of love, pain, memory, and ultimately the miracle of survival. Her intensely alive, lyrical, and fearless writing is electric with prescient urgency, wavering between sorrow and joy whilst retaining a hypnotic heart.

    —Candice Louisa Daquin, author of *Tainted by the Same Counterfeit*

Melissa Fadul's debut collection *Pulse* is a deeply moving exploration of girlhood, gender, sex, and social justice. In poems that both elegize and celebrate, Fadul bears witness to histories of violence, from the Holocaust to Stonewall to the murder of Matthew Shepard to the struggles of high school students in the speaker's New York City classrooms. *Pulse* is a book of historical reckoning and personal experience—a beautiful, urgent collection.

    —Nicole Cooley

About the Author

Melissa Fadul has been published in a wide array of anthologies and poetry magazines. In 2020, *Negative Capability Press*, selected her poem, "Tattooist's Needle, Jewish Museum" for honorable mention in their spring contest. Melissa holds an MFA from *Sarah Lawrence College*, an MA from *Queens College* and a BA from the *New School University*.

Melissa has been teaching for twenty years. She has taught in *New York* and *London* where she lived for two years. Currently, she is going into her thirteenth year serving as one of the founding English teachers at a high school in *New York*. She lives in New York with her wife and three furry loves: Roggie her adorable bunny and Linus and Izzy her Maltese babies who run the household. *Pulse* is her first collection of poetry. She can be contacted at: melissafadul@gmail.com.